Guest Name &
Address

AF094585

Thoughts & Best Wishes

Thoughts & Best Wishes

Guest Name & Address

Guest Name & Address

Thoughts & Best Wishes

Guest Name & Address

Guest Name & Address

Guest Name & Address

Thoughts & Best Wishes

Guest Name & Address

Guest Name & Address

Guest Name & Address

Guest Name & Address

Guest Name & Address

Guest Name & Address

Thoughts & Best Wishes

Guest Name & Address

Thoughts & Best Wishes

Thoughts & Best Wishes

Guest Name & Address

Thoughts & Best Wishes

Guest Name & Address

Thoughts & Best Wishes

Thoughts & Best Wishes

Guest Name & Address

Thoughts & Best Wishes

Guest Name & Address

Thoughts & Best Wishes

Guest Name & Address

Thoughts & Best Wishes

Guest Name & Address

Thoughts & Best Wishes

Guest Name & Address

Guest Name & Address

Thoughts & Best Wishes

Guest Name & Address

Guest Name & Address

Guest Name & Address

Guest Name & Address

Guest Name & Address

Thoughts & Best Wishes

Guest Name & Address

Thoughts & Best Wishes

Guest Name & Address

Thoughts & Best Wishes

Guest Name & Address

Thoughts & Best Wishes

Guest Name & Address

Thoughts & Best Wishes

Guest Name & Address

Guest Name & Address

Thoughts & Best Wishes

Guest Name & Address

Guest Name & Address

Guest Name & Address

Guest Name & Address

Guest Name & Address

Guest Name & Address

Guest Name & Address

Thoughts & Best Wishes

Guest Name & Address

www.ingramcontent.com/pod-product-compliance
Lightning Source LLC
LaVergne TN
LVHW060159080526
838202LV00052B/4172